Freshwater Fish
Walleyed Pike

Launch!
An Imprint of Abdo Zoom
abdopublishing.com

Leo Statts

abdopublishing.com

Published by Abdo Zoom, a division of ABDO, PO Box 398166, Minneapolis, Minnesota 55439.
Copyright © 2019 by Abdo Consulting Group, Inc. International copyrights reserved in all countries.
No part of this book may be reproduced in any form without written permission from the publisher.
Launch!™ is a trademark and logo of Abdo Zoom.

Printed in the United States of America, North Mankato, Minnesota.

052018
092018

**THIS BOOK CONTAINS
RECYCLED MATERIALS**

Photo Credits: Engbretson Underwater Photography, iStock, Shutterstock

Production Contributors: Kenny Abdo, Jennie Forsberg, Grace Hansen, John Hansen

Design Contributors: Dorothy Toth, Neil Klinepier

Library of Congress Control Number: 2017960626

Publisher's Cataloging-in-Publication Data

Names: Statts, Leo, author.

Title: Walleyed pike / by Leo Statts.

Description: Minneapolis, Minnesota : Abdo Zoom, 2019. | Series: Freshwater fish |
    Includes online resources and index.

Identifiers: ISBN 9781532122934 (lib.bdg.) | ISBN 9781532123917 (ebook) |
    ISBN 9781532124402 (Read-to-me ebook)

Subjects: LCSH: Walleye (Fish)--Juvenile literature. | Freshwater fishes--Juvenile literature. |
    Walleyed pike--Juvenile literature. | Fishes--Juvenile literature.

Classification: DDC 597.092--dc23

Table of Contents

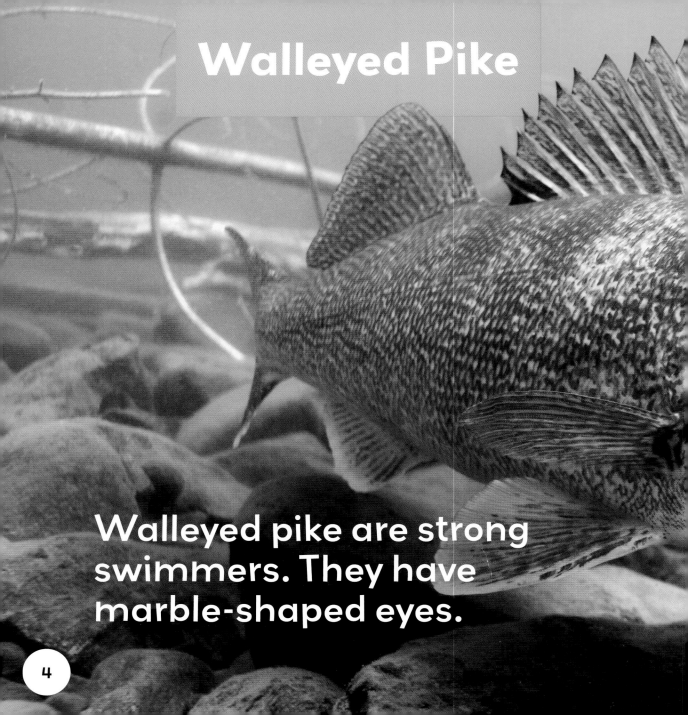

Walleyed Pike

Walleyed pike are strong swimmers. They have marble-shaped eyes.

Their eyes let them see in dark water. This helps them catch prey.

Body

Walleyed pike have teeth. Their long, thin bodies are covered in **scales**.

They are brownish-green in color. Some have silver backs and white undersides.

Walleyed pike live in **freshwater** lakes and rivers.

Walleyed pike swim in deep, dark water. They avoid the sun.

They use rocks, sunken trees, and weeds to hide.

Food

Walleyed pike are **carnivores**.

They eat insects, snails, and other fish.

They hold prey with their teeth.

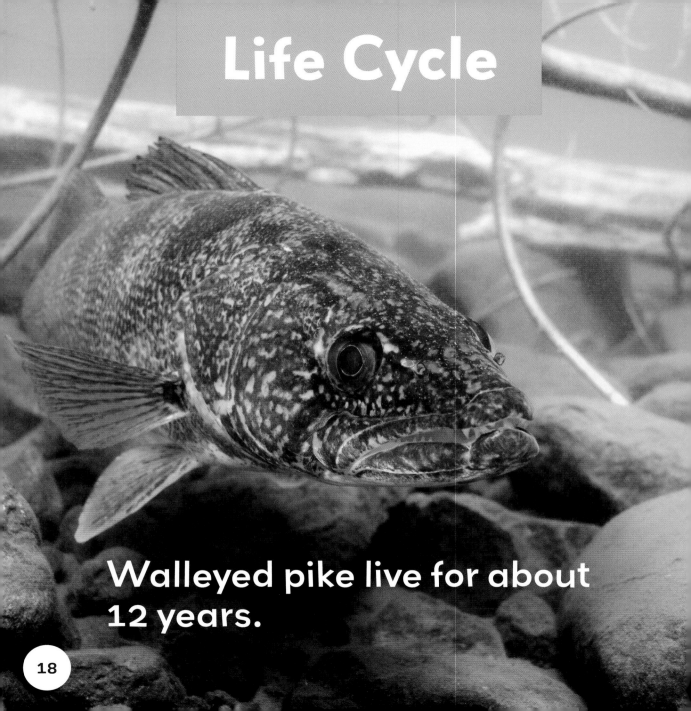

Life Cycle

Walleyed pike live for about 12 years.

They lay eggs in rocky areas. The eggs stick to rocks and weeds. This protects them until they **hatch**.

Average Weight

A walleyed pike is lighter than a bowling ball.

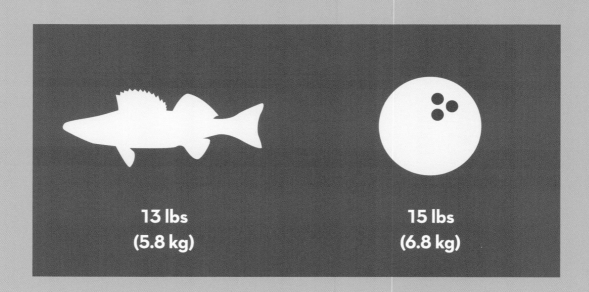

13 lbs
(5.8 kg)

15 lbs
(6.8 kg)

Average Length

A walleyed pike is shorter than an acoustic guitar.

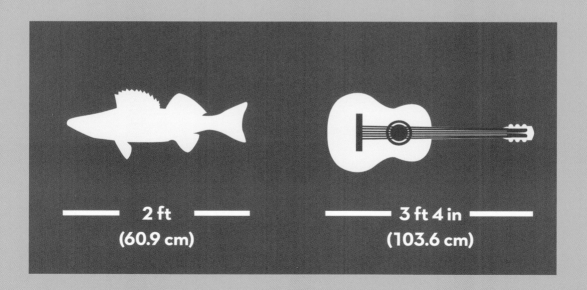

2 ft
(60.9 cm)

3 ft 4 in
(103.6 cm)

Glossary

carnivore – an animal that eats meat.

freshwater – consisting of or containing fresh water.

hatch – to be born from an egg.

prey – an animal hunted or killed by a predator for food.

scales – flat plates that form the outer covering of fish.

Online Resources

For more information on
walleyed pike, please visit
abdobooklinks.com

Learn even more with the
Abdo Zoom Animals database.
Visit **abdozoom.com** today!

Index